Levels and Curves with GIMP
Second Edition

Alberto García Briz

Levels and Curves with GIMP
Alberto García Briz

Second Edition

Paperback version:
  ISBN-13: 978-1503229853 (CreateSpace)
  ISBN-10: 1503229858

Once again, to Silvia and Gabriela

Contents

Levels and Curves with GIMP

Introduction

Since a few years now, I am editing a couple of blogs on image edition – mostly, with GIMP, a free application with Open Source license. I even published a book (you can see the details at the end of this one) on the conversion to black and white with that program.

During the preparation of these publications I realized the importance and power of curves adjustment in photographic edition. Maybe as important as to dedicate a whole book on this… if you can read this, it means I was right.

Of course, curves adjustment is closely related to how digital information is created, calculated and stored. And there is a relationship to information tools such as the histogram. As a consequence, these concepts have also been incorporated here, in order to provide a global overview of the tool…

Maybe you have a too complex book in your hands? Not needed? I hope some people will find it useful… Anyway, I tried to use plain language, with down-to-earth expressions, introducing the concepts in a logical line of thought, to reach that global view of the presented tools.

Some of the texts presented here are adapted both from my book and blogs (if you have time, just check http://albertog.over-blog.es and http://albertogblog.blogspot.com). But of course, different sources were also used from the Internet, such as the great blog by Petteri Sulonen (http://www.prime-junta.net, check the "How to" section).

I tried to keep a simple layout towards the publication as eBook and PDF document. But you might be reading the paper version, with some more details for those who still prefer "real hardware"…

About this edition

One of the topics I referred to in the first edition of this book, which was not really explained, was the use of masks; even when they are not strictly needed, they can help in simplifying the edition process, by limiting the areas affected by our curves or levels edition.

With this in mind, I prepared (for the second edition of this book, in Spanish) a new specific section. This forced me to treat is as a fully new book, since it was an important edition and the number of pages (and so the ISBN) was also affected. Little by little, I achieved to remove the original book from the market.

Regarding physical format, the second Spanish edition was produced in a slightly smaller size that the original version, to facilitate handing and postage.

However, this new format (five by eight inches) was not a standard for colour books in bookshops. This reduced strongly the commercial possibilities. So I decide to go back to the "Statement" format (5.5 by 8.5 inches) of the current paperback version. In parallel, I made some style and writing correction.

By reducing font sizes, the increase in contents did not affect the number of pages in the paperback version, so that final price was also not affected (which is good: this book is printed on demand).

Digital images

Nowadays, we can find digital cameras almost everywhere. What just a decade ago was limited to computer work, has been universalized by the Internet and the possibility of printing onto almost any desired support.

You could also say that everyone in a developed country has access to a digital camera (with better or poorer quality...), at least to the ones included in most modern cell phones. So the possibility of creating digital images is there, for good or for bad.

But, in many cases, the limitations on the camera or the captured scene will result in images that do not match our expectations. In many cases, we may want to improve them, to share them with our online contacts, or rather to prepare collages or specific documents.

A modern cell phone can generate files with some kinds of edition, such as cropping and colouring (here, a sepia tint)

Of course, many smart phones do include edition apps that allow you to modify your pictures "on the fly", so that basic edition can be applied on the very handset: change to black and white or sepia, simulation of old film pictures...

And many edition programs such as GIMP, used in this book, include automated functions for quick edition, developed to avoid many headaches – but also a share of creative possibilities.

7

In this book we will see how to handle digital information in order to produce results closer to our expectations, closer to the planned scene we wanted to capture – or rather, more spectacular and appealing.

We will also see the way to automate (up to some extent) "our" personal editions, so that we can recall and apply them in a later edition to the same picture – or to a different one.

Points and pixels

Main concept that we need to understand is that digital images are made of points with a single colour. Those points are referred to as pixels (from PICture ELement). They are defined by their colour, and they are the smallest information piece possible in a picture.

Above: Any digital image is made of "square" points with a single colour (pixel). We can always see them, by zooming in to the maximum...

> *Notice: a very useful keyboard shortcut in GIMP is the zoom tool, which allows for zooming-in (by pressing "+") and out (with the key "-")*

Of course, we need to have a way to "see" those pixels, either on the screen or out from a printer.

And we will find that, in order to show a single pixel, a monitor will use three or four light points (from the three primary colours, red, green and blue) with different intensities. And a printer may need thousands of microscopic ink droplets in a specific area, of different colours, to produce the desired colour.

So we face a first "possible confusion": if we speak about points, are we referring to image ones, to dots in a screen, ink droplets...?

Typically (and this is what we will do from now on in this book), information points in an image are referred to as "pixels", then "points" is used for output devices (monitors, printers) that render those pixels. Usually, we will have a given number of points to create a single pixel.

Bits and Bytes

From the above situation, how does a computer handle pixels? Well, when working with an image, a computer will create an imaginary grid, overlaid to the image, so that each cell will contain a single pixel.

Then, we will be able to know the information from each pixel if we know two key data: the position of the pixel in the grid (vertical and horizontal coordinates) and the value assigned for the contained colour.

It is easy to imagine how to manage the coordinates system, from one corner (Usually, the lower left one). On the contrary, it will be more complex to define how to store each different colour as digital information. And here is where digital data comes in, as bits and bytes.

In Computing, a bit is the smallest information unit possible. Electronic circuits will store and transmit signals in two different levels, so that we can differentiate them. A bit of information will indicate one of those levels. It will be "A" or "B", "high" or "low", black or white... Usual convention is to use the binary numeric system, which will only use the numbers zero and one.

Furthermore, most edition programs will follow a same rule, quite useful: "zero" indicates absence of colour (thus typically black), then one indicates "full" colour – white (or the specific primary colour).

But this does not provide much freedom to store our information, if (together with the coordinates) we can just say if a pixel has colour or not.

The way to overcome this is to use more digits to define the information of each point. If we use two bits per pixel, we can produce four different combinations, and thus we can define the following:

00 – Black
01 – Dark Grey
10 – Light Grey
11 – White

If we used three bits per pixel, we would have eight different combinations. With four bits per pixel, 16 possibilities... take a look at the following table to see how we can build some greyscale tones from binary combinations.

Definición de colores con 3 bits

dec	bits	% color	valor	color
0	000	0,00%	0	
1	001	14,29%	36	
2	010	28,57%	73	
3	011	42,86%	109	
4	100	57,14%	146	
5	101	71,43%	182	
6	110	85,71%	219	
7	111	100,00%	255	

Definición de colores con 4 bits

dec	bits	%	valor	color
0	0000	0,00%	0	
1	0001	6,67%	17	
2	0010	13,33%	34	
3	0011	20,00%	51	
4	0100	26,67%	68	
5	0101	33,33%	85	
6	0110	40,00%	102	
7	0111	46,67%	119	
8	1000	53,33%	136	
9	1001	60,00%	153	
10	1010	66,67%	170	
11	1011	73,33%	187	
12	1100	80,00%	204	
13	1101	86,67%	221	
14	1110	93,33%	238	
15	1111	100,00%	255	

Definition of greyscale tones with three and four bits. Adapted from
Blanco y Negro con The GIMP, Alberto García Briz

A commonly used data structure in Computing is the Byte, equivalent to eight bits. Many microcontrollers and microprocessors are designed to work with these 8-bit blocks, or groups of those (16, 32, 64 bits...)

If we follow the previous process, we could represent up to 256 different greyscale tones (for example, black, white and 254 intermediate tones). This amount of different tones is already enough to produce nice viewing results; human eye will scarcely detect transitions between two consecutive tones.

Still one step forward, human eye is sensitive to three primary colours, red, green and blue. If we could define the right proportion of those, we could represent any desired colour with high accuracy.

The RGB system uses, for example, that strategy (additive colours) and it uses three bytes to define each pixel, one byte per primary colour (also referred to one byte per colour *channel*).

With 256 combinations per channel, we can produce more than 17 million different colours… enough to show any "normal" photography. IN fact, this is the system used by most display devices…

Left: Image in GIF format, using eight bits per pixel. **Right**: the same image using 24 bits per pixel. Source: **Blanco y Negro con The GIMP, Alberto García Briz**

Of course, printing and professional imaging systems can be far more complex. They can use even more bits of information per pixel (12 or 16 per channel, thus 36 or 48 per pixel), but those are very specific applications.

And there are also some image formats that use less bits per pixel, either because they use alternative strategies (such as colour indexing) or because the total number of colours to render is limited, which, in principle, should produce images with lower quality.

Current eBook readers (if you are reading the electronic version, this might be your case) typically work with four bits per pixel, so they can only render 16 different greyscale tones.

Limits and trimming

So far it is enough for us to know that all pixels in our image can use values from zero to 255, either as greyscale value or per each primary colour channel.

Specifically, we will never have negative values, nor higher than 255. This will limit our edition actions, "trimming" some colour areas if we apply some strong change.

If we try to produce too light values, out of range, our edition program will limit (trim) that to 255 (maximum value), avoiding any higher value. This will translate into areas with uniform, white colour. These may not be comfortable to look at, since they may provide a wrong information that "something is missing" in the picture.

If, on the contrary, we try to obtain negative values ("more black than black"), the program will just assign the value "zero" to the affected pixels, trimming the data to black colour. In this case, we will see uniform, black areas without any useful image information (contours, texture).

The histogram

The Histogram is a graphic representation of the amount of pixels in an image with a given colour value.

To begin with, we will use a very simple "image", including sixteen different points with shades of 8-bit grey (this is called greyscale):

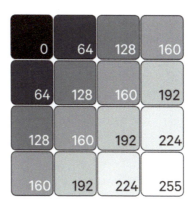

On each pixel, I have included the numeric value for the specific tone. Note that zero indicates pure black, whereas 255 is assigned to pure white. All intermediate tones will have values between those two, being lighter as the value is higher.

Now, I create a list of the tones in my image, together with the number of times that these values are used:

Value	Amount
0	1
64	2
128	3
160	4
192	3
224	2
255	1

Now, we can produce a first graph to show this information, as follows:

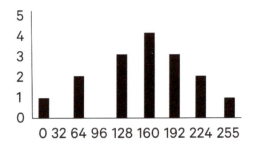

Notice that I put the lowest values (zero being pure black) on the left, then highest values (up to 255, pure white) on the right. In the vertical axis, we put the number of pixels containing each value. In this simplified example, there is no pixel (amount = 0) with value 32, nor 96.

Well, this simple graphic is our histogram. Of course, the image is far too simple. A "normal" picture in greyscale will have pixels with any of the 256 different values, from pure black to pure white.

Besides, a typical image will contain pixels with all (or most) values; if there is a predominant tone or shade, we will see an outstanding column or "peak" for that specific value.

Since it is not practical to write all 256 values on the lower axis, those are usually not written at all. In GIMP, you can see the histogram of an opened picture by using the command "Colours – Info – Histogram":

In the previous picture, we see a peak on the lightest values (right of the graph), corresponding to the light background. On the contrary, there are no points on the left side. This means that pure black is not present in our picture. Only dark grey tones are present.

Apart from that, we can also see a uniform distribution of the remaining tones. In our case, those are the shades of grey of the lion's fur, and the post behind it.

Types of Histograms

From the very definition of the histogram, we will be able to use it as an analysis tool, to check how numeric information is distributed in our image, detect any possible problem and find out how to solve it. Usually, we will check two different things:

There should not be a big amount of pixels on the extreme values, either black or white. Except in some specific image types (high or low key), this would mean wide areas filled with white or black, without any detail, texture or image information.

As we indicated, we would say that the image is "trimmed" in the highlights or in the shadows, respectively.

A uniform distribution along the graph may not produce (as you might think) a nice result. Instead, we might prefer to work with images showing one or several peaks of information at specific tones.

So usually we will find one of the following histogram types:

> **Single peak on the right side:** This corresponds to a mostly clear image, typically a high-key one, or rather well lit or with clear objects. It can be the case of a picture taken in a snowy landscape, or at the beach. We face the risk of "burning" the highlights, losing details in the clearest zones. We should avoid peaks above the 245 mark, as a reference.

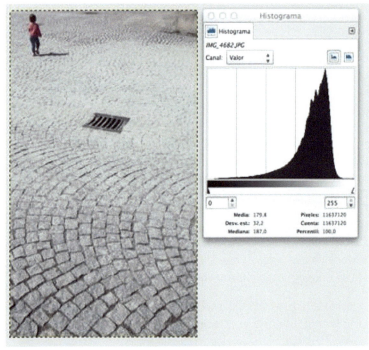

Above: Image with high contents of clear tones (high values). Notice that there are no points with highest or lowest values (pure white or black, respectively)

Single peak on the left side: Opposite to the previous one, this is valid in low-key images, or when captured objects are dark. Again, we should avoid having the peak on the zero value – say, from value 10 upwards, to eliminate the risk of losing information (textures, shapes) in the shadows.

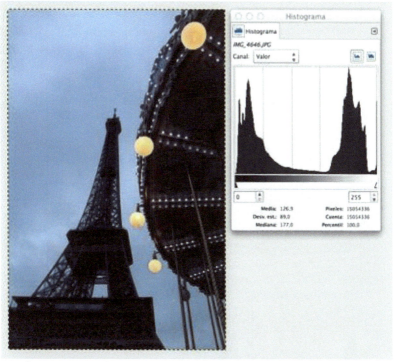

Above: image with two clear peaks, one in the shadows (tower, merry-go-round) and another one in the lights (sky, decoration lights). Here we do have some trimming in the pure white, since the camera over-exposed the small bulbs...

Two peaks, one in the highlights and the other in the shadows: Previous image would be an example for this. Preliminarily, this would be an image with high contrast, which could be positive. Again, peaks should not be too close to the limits, since now we would lose information on both extremes.

Anyway, a lack of intermediate tones (values too low between the peaks) may produce "uneasy" pictures, not really nice to look at...

Of course, it is very different to have sharp peaks (limited to a few values) or wide ones, with values softly descending to the sides. First case might be, for example, a low-key portrait with some shiny elements, such as the eyes, teeth or some jewellery.

17

Histogram per channel

If we find that our image has some wrong tint, or a tone that we would like to correct (maybe a yellowish image taken under bulb light, or bluish because of fluorescent lighting), we can also analyse each colour channel (red, green or blue) separately.

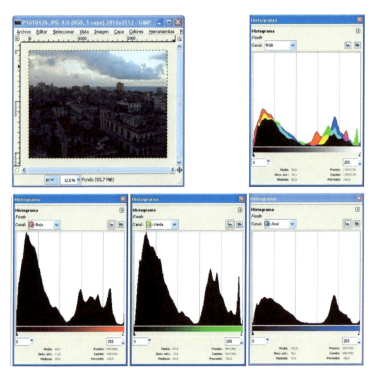

Composite RGB histogram and per colour channel. You can see that each channel has different value information. Source: **Blanco y Negro con The GIMP**, Alberto García Briz

To do so, you must select the desired cannel from the drop-down menu in the histogram window. As default, the "Value" (average from all three channels) is selected and shown in the histogram.

As a practical tip, the gradient under the graph will change to the selected colour – so we can easily identify which channel is presented in the graph. We will be able to detect if there is any trimming in the highlights or shadows of the active channel, for example.

Basic calculations

Well, so we have our 4 x 4 image, and we produced its histogram. What can we do from there? Of course, play with those values.

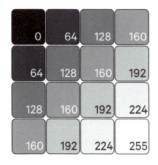 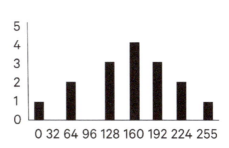

If we add or subtract a given number (for example, 32) to all points, we will get a lighter or darker image, respectively:

 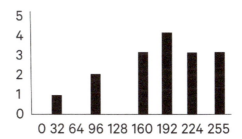

All obtained values over 255 will be trimmed, as we saw before.

We can also see that the values distribution has shifted to the right, and we do not have any more pixels with values zero, 64 or 128. Value 255 has more importance (more "weight") now, due to the increase of trimmed pixels.

Alternatively we could multiply (or divide) all values in the image. If we multiply by two, we would get the following image as a result:

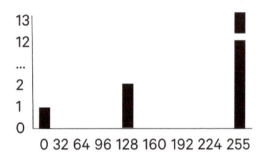

Division by a number greater than one would produce a completely different result, with the special characteristic that no negative value is produced, nor any value higher than 255, so no trimming would occur.

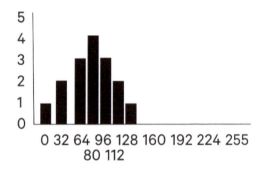

We can see that division (or multiplication by a number smaller than one) produces a concentration of values on the left side, where darker tones are located.

All the above modifications have been applied to the whole image. The full set of values has shifted uniformly "upwards" (addition, multiplication) or "downwards" (subtraction, division).

Notice that operations that increase the pixels' values will produce lighter images, whereas any calculation that produces lower values will output darker images. In many cases, these simple transformations can help in moving away from trimming thresholds, "moving" our pixel values to the intermediate grey values.

But we need to work carefully: a high value used in any calculation to get away from one extreme of the histogram may produce a trim in the opposite end, and the final image would lose detail anyway…

In the previous examples, by multiplying we obtained "too many" points with value 255, so most of the image information was lost. And this information cannot be recovered back.

Anyway, we just saw a "mathematical" way to lighten (or darken) an image. We start to see how we can influence the information contained in a picture – even without considering the "real" image content.

Considering an image to be just a grid of "meaningless" values is a good exercise to begin with... but with a bigger picture, containing several million pixels, we will not perform any manual calculation – will we?

> *Notice: When we invert the colors in an image, GIMP will produce the new value by subtracting the original from 255. This way, white color (255) will produce 255 – 255 = 0 (pure black) and black will output 255 – 0 = 255 (white).*
>
> *A dark grey (for example, 64) will produce a lighter one (255 – 64 = 191) and so on...*

Levels adjustment

Of course, the question is, can I do these transformations with an image editor? And, if so, how does GIMP do it? Answer is, with the Levels adjustment.

But the way to work will be slightly different: we will not have the opportunity to input the value to be added or subtracted (or multiplied, divided…). Instead, we will define what "is" for us white colour, and what is black. And some grey in between…

Levels tool

In GIMP, with any open image, we can select the command "*Colours – Levels…*" to open the following dialog window:

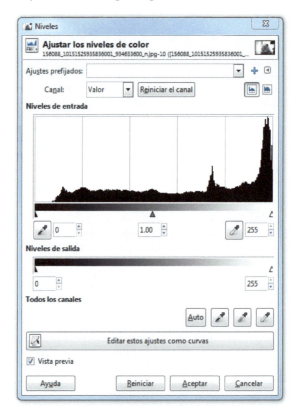

By now, we will not consider the information on the upper area. In the centre, you can see the histogram of your image (well!), which typically will show a certain distribution of values between both extremes. Maybe you will see one or two peaks.

Right underneath, there is a gradient bar (form black to white) with three triangles, indicating the position of black, mid grey and white.

Black and white colours are also shown with their numeric value (initially, zero and 255). We can also see some colour pickers (again, black, grey and white). Don't do anything yet...

A bit below, you find another gradient bar, labelled as "Output levels". This gradient has two triangles and also numeric input values.

Under that, a button labelled as "Edit the adjustment as curves". You can imagine this is related to the curves tool – but we will see this later on.

Finally, you will see a checkbox to preview the changes, and the usual buttons for Apply, Cancel and Help, together with a Reset button, to begin from the starting position, if we get somehow lost...

Definition of input points

First step will be to "tell GIMP" what is white and what is black in our picture.

Dark image...

In some cases, you will have images with most of their information on one side – and fewer on the opposite one. This may simply mean that you are (willingly) not using all available tones. El primer paso será el de "decirle" a GIMP qué es el color blanco y el negro en nuestra imagen.

Well, this could be right. You may capture a scene without bright objects, or dark shadows. In that case, the picture might be valid. However, usually we will try that our images use as much tonal range as possible, to produce nicer images.

Then, having a reference of some bright and dark objects in the image can help us in "locating" all intermediate tones.

For example, I will consider the following picture, taken at dusk with little ambient light. No direct sunlight, also no reflections or shines to be highlighted. In general, it gives a "dark" impression – in fact, it was quite late in the afternoon…

Now, I open the auxiliary window for levels adjustment with "*Colours – Levels…*"

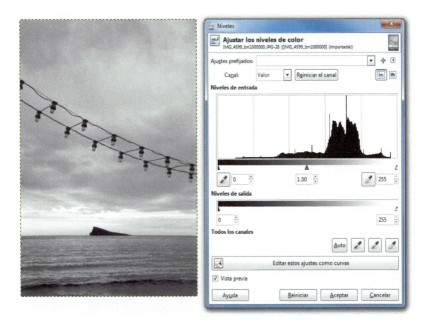

We can see that there is almost no information on the right side of the histogram, which means that there are NO white pixels in the image. And this is right.

However, to improve the look of the image, we will force it to contain white colour, by dragging the white triangle in the upper gradient to the left (in this example, down to the value 245):

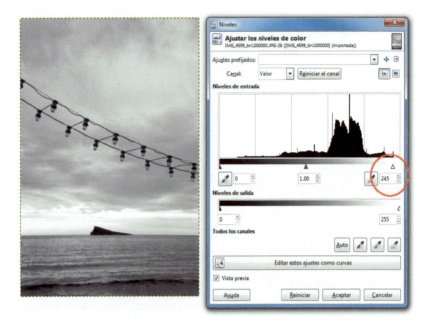

By doing this adjustment, the whole image has been lightened up slightly.

> **Math:** ¿What does this value mean? In fact, we are multiplying all values in our picture by 255/245 = 1.04 (all values rounded to the closest integer). So we are lightening the whole image – including the darkest areas. Black colour will remain black, since 0 x 1.04 = 0.

Anyway, if you open the histogram now ("*Colours – Info – Histogram*") you will see that we stretched the values to include pure white, but (since we are rounding the results) some values will not be present at all, producing white "empty" bars in the histogram.

Actually, because of that multiplication-and-rounding process we arrive to some new values (not all of them), so we are still not using the full range of tones. We just redistributed them to produce a nicer result...

And this has to be clear: you are not creating new information, but redistributing the set of values. It is up to you to decide which *distribution* looks better to you. Either the original, dark one (but real, made at dusk) or the new, clearer one...

Bright image...

If we have the opposite situation, a too-bright image without information on the darkest shadows, we could drag the black triangle towards the left side, usually up to the position where we do have values different than zero.

I will reuse the lion picture from previous sections. As I commented, it does not contain pure black. Values start around grey tone 15 (quite dark anyway...).

In this case, we "pull" the light towards the left side, so the overall image gets darker. We have a new numeric value for pure black (in this case, I set it to 20).

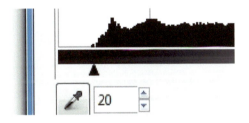

White colour is not affected, like all brighter values. Now, check the difference between both images:

Above: Original image, no pure black is used. Below: Edited image with modified levels.

The introduced change is minimum. However, you might see some contrast improvement in the mid tones, for example in the fur. As a side effect, leaves in the foreground, snout and mouth are darker now, too.

> **Math:** *In this case, it is a bit more complex. First, we subtract the selected value (20) from all points (so we add an overall darkening) and then we multiply the result by 255/(255-20). So white colour remains white, since (255-20) * 255/(255-20) = 255.*

As you can see in the example picture (maybe it lacked some contrast, it was too "soft"), we can recover part of the image contrast even when we are not creating new information. We are redistributing values, just as in the previous section.

Back to the example of the beach picture, we can also see that it did not have pure black, either. We should also try to correct this…

In this case, I move the black triangle up to the value 25 (remember: first values with valid information in the histogram). By applying both changes, (white to 245, black to 25), the new image will contain both extremes – but at a cost, we will have lost some intermediate value.

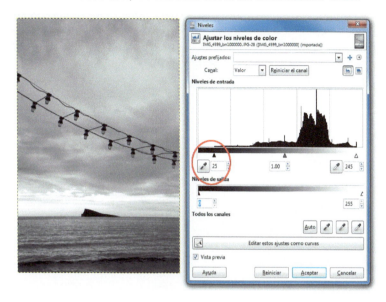

If our edition is subtle, the effect will not be noticed, but the image will usually be enhanced. If the edition is too strong, we might see some pattern generation or banding effects – something unpleasant, since we are adding artificial structures or information to the picture.

Droppers

A straight way to work with levels adjustment is to pick our reference white and black levels directly from the image by means of the droppers.

For each colour (black, white and also grey) there is one specific dropper. By clicking on each button, the mouse cursor will change accordingly. Then, all you have to do is to click on the picture, in the area where you consider the white (or black, or grey...) colour to be. The information on that pixel will be used in the levels tool.

Droppers may not be as exact as the numeric input (for you might have slight tone changes in an area that seems to be uniform). However, they can be a good first approach to get starting values. Furthermore, by clicking in different areas you may see the immediate effect of picking one tone or another...

Middle point...

Once we have chosen our black and white points (either by moving the triangles, by directly inputting numeric values or through the droppers), we can define the *behaviour* of the mid tones with the grey triangle.

This indicates the ratio between lights and shadows. Initially, it is set at a value of 128, and numeric input indicates "1.00". There is the same amount of clear tones (126 plus pure white) than dark ones (126 plus pure black) at both sides of this point:

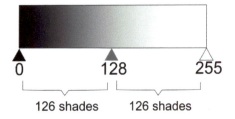

If we move the slider to the left, we decide to have *fewer* tones below 128. On the contrary, many points will take values lighter than 128. Ratio between light and dark tones will now be higher than one, so the numeric value will be higher than 1.00.

Resulting image will be lighter, and we will have lost some detail in the shadows (now, we will not have all values between 0 and 128), and also in the highlights (some points will take identical high values).

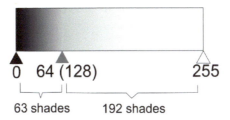

63 shades   192 shades

On the contrary, if we move the 128 reference to the right, we allow for fewer tones between 128 and 255, and many pixels will now take values between 0 and 128:

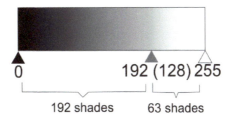

192 shades   63 shades

In this case, fraction will be less than 1.00, and the final image will look darker. Again, we are losing some information from the image, since we will be duplicating some dark tones and reducing the number of different light ones.

Definition of output points

So far, we have seen how to get our image to look good on the screen (and later on, when printing). However, displays and printers do have some technical limitations, which will produce some issues when producing the output.

Black...

Specifically, it will be quite complicated to show the differences between two very dark tones, close to pure black. In monitors, this means almost full absence of light (either by masking it in TFT screens or not emitting it at all in LED ones), and we will work around the limits of the device.

With printers, it is even worse, because black colour is produced by the application of a certain amount of toner powder (which is melt to provide an even finish), or rather of ink droplets (which spread over the paper surface before drying). High contents of pigments get difficult to control in the limits of the range.

This way, a possible solution is not to use pure black when printing. We will force the printer to use darker or lighter greys, but no pure black. So we avoid using the "full" amount of pigment on any area.

> *Notice*: In professional printing, CMYK system is used (see glossary at the end of the book). Only seldom will be pure black used. Instead, percentages of other colours are used, to provide the black with certain characteristics. This way, we might find definitions such as:
>
> - *Standard black* (0C, 0M, 0Y, 100K)
> - *Cool black* (60C, 0M, 0Y, 100K)
> - *Warm black* (0C, 60M, 30Y, 100K)
> - *Neutral Black* (50C, 50M, 50Y, 100K)...
>
> GIMP cannot work directly with the CMYK system. However, you may use the above values to define RGB approximate equivalents...

The way to limit the pure black output when printing is to use the lower gradient tool in the Levels window. Black triangle has to be dragged to the right, to define which value for dark grey is our limit for "dark" output in the printer – for example, a value between five and ten.

...and white

Similarly, when rendering very clear tones, close to pure white, we may produce empty areas in our pictures or on the screen. It feels like "something is missing", even when it is not so.

The way to avoid this is limiting our "brightest white", making GIMP show some information on screen – or in our prints. We will define a very clear grey to be that limit.

Moving the lower white triangle to the left, we will get all tones above the defined limit to be represented as this limit. A distance of 5 to 10 points from the maximum 255 is also a good approach. So we will set a value (for example) of 245 or 250.

Above: without a proper frame, the burned sky may give the impression that something is missing in the upper areas of the image...

Clarifications...

In the Levels adjustment window we can also see an "Auto" button, which will produce an automated first approach to levels correction, as per GIMP *opinion*. Try to open any image and use this button. In most cases, the result will be already quite good...

But here is where a right screen and printer calibration is needed. As I say, most of the times the automatic adjustment will be just right. You might want to fine-tune it, a few points to the left or right. But not much more. If you do not see a nice picture on your screen, this might mean that it is not properly adjusted, or you ambient light conditions are not ideal.

And a similar thing will happen to your printer. A "perfect" picture on your screen can produce horrible results in print. The way computer drivers mix the different pigments (either solid or liquid) and the specific proportion to reach a given colour might give you many a surprise...

At the end of this book we will see a basic method to calibrate a printer with the curves adjustment.

Levels adjustment per channel

As we saw in the histogram chapter, we can see the separate colour distribution in each primary colour cannel (red, green and blue).

And we can use this information, indeed. In the Levels adjustment window, you have (in the upper part) a drop-down menu, which lets you select which channel to edit. If you train enough, you may use these channels to correct slight colour tints (typically, just by moving the central triangle).

Anyway, if we adjust a channel separately we may miss (or displace) the colour balance in the whole picture. You can arrive to some really interesting, artistic results. Or you might also ruin a nice picture... remember always to work with copies of your original pictures.

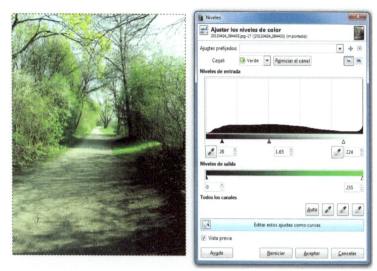

Above: Example of channel edition. Highlights have been lowered (to avoid lights clipping because of saturation), shadows have been lightened (to eliminate black areas) and middle point has been shifter to the left, to give more importance to light tones.

Save your settings...

The default configuration of GIMP does not contain any levels adjustment. You can see a drop-down menu labelled as "stored settings", which is empty.

If you have a series of pictures taken with similar lighting conditions or camera settings, you may store some specific setting to apply it to all of them.

The way to do this will be to lick on the "+" icon, visible next to this drop-down menu. GIMP will prompt you for a name for that setting. After storing it, you will be able to recall it at any time – and with any picture.

Levels - conclusions...

Well, Levels adjustment is useful to edit our images and "save" some information on the highlights or shadows... It is a simple tool, which provides certain flexibility and "takes into account our opinion" on how the image should look like. We can decide if it has to be darker, clearer, or how grey tones should be distributed.

Of course, adjusting the mid grey has the risk of losing some image information, so this adjustment must be done carefully.

Furthermore, we can correct (up to some extent) the output of our image (either on screen or in print) to make it nicer to view, keeping details both in lights and in shadows.

But still this is a rigid method to modify the tones or colours in an image, especially the mid tones... Maybe if the tool provided two (or three, or more...) intermediate grey settings, we might further fine-tune our pictures... Then, is there any other way, other tool, to correct lighting in our photos?

Curves adjustment

Answer is yes, the tool does exist. And it is, of course, the Curves adjustment. It follows a similar *philosophy* as Levels adjustment, but it provides one step further in adjustment freedom. In theory, we might use a different modification (addition, multiplication...) factor for each separate tone in the original image.

Or rather, we will be able, for example, to select a given range of values and modify their value, increasing them (lightening the pixels) or reducing them (darkening). Or maybe we can propose a transformation that is stronger in the highlights and just slight in the shadows...

Curves tool

We can show the auxiliary window for curves adjustment by using the command "Colours – Curves..." with an open image. Working environment will be quite similar to that of the Levels adjustment.

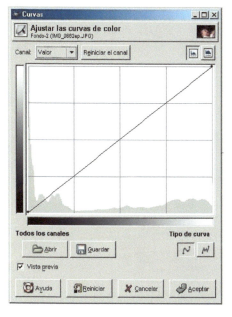

Main difference will be, of course, the addition of the curve in the centre of this window. Initially, the "curve" will be a diagonal line overlaid on the histogram of our image. Two gradients are added, one underneath the histogram, the other to the left side.

On this diagonal, we can also see two small points (or squares, depending on your Operating System) on both extremes.

Interpretation of the initial curve

OK. So you can see this diagonal. You see the gradients, the two squares... but, what are you actually seeing?

This diagonal line (remember, it is our starting curve) shows the correspondence between the original image and the output one, after applying (if any) the transformation.

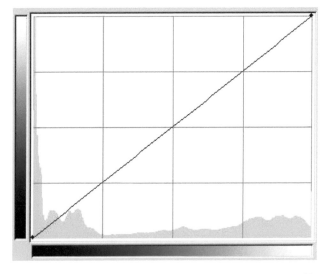

So the small square down left indicates that black colour (from the **below** gradient) is in fact black (on the **left** gradient).

And the control square on top right indicates that white colour (from the **below** gradient) will output white colour (from the **left** gradient).

Finally, any intermediate grey will output the same shade of grey. At least, initially. Now, let's see how to change this...

Moving control points

With the mouse we can drag these small squares all around the histogram. By now, we will do something easy: move them along the borders of the histogram.

> *Notice*: *The images used in this section are adapted from the book "**Blanco y Negro con The GIMP**", from the same author.*

If we move the black point control to the right, we are indicating that a given grey tone from the below gradient (remember, that is our original image) must output pure black. Any darker shade of grey will also take that value:

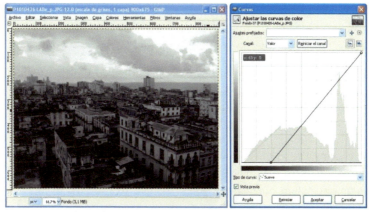

Above: black control point is displaced to the right

We just darkened the image, just as when we adjusted levels by moving the black triangle to the right. Here you can see in a graphical way what is happening to mid tones.

The new diagonal is below the original one, and overall tones are darker. Remember, form the levels adjustment, that we are losing image information, since a number of pixels (all below the selected value) now get the value zero. Later editions will not be able to differentiate them to recover any texture, for example.

If we moved the black control point upwards, we would force all points with original black value to get a lighter value, the selected one in the left (target) gradient. All other tones will adapt to the new conditions.

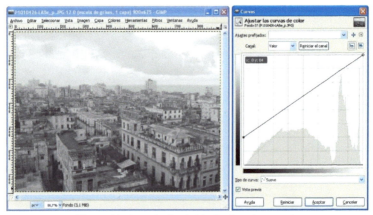

Above: black control point is displaced upwards

Again, we are losing information since, we will only use the values above the selected grey shade, and not the available 256 different ones.

If we move the white control point we will arrive to similar situations. Moving it on the horizontal axis, we assign the value 255 to all shades in the original picture which are above the selected point. Once again, all values are adapted to this new boundary condition.

By assigning the value 255 to many pixels in our image, we are losing information on the highlights. This happened also with levels adjustment, when moving the white triangle to the left. In fact, it is exactly the same transformation.

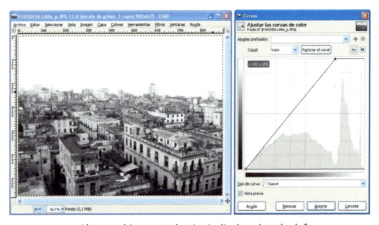

Above: white control point is displaced to the left

Finally, if we drag the white control point downwards we are limiting the highest values in the output, so the image will be darkened in general.

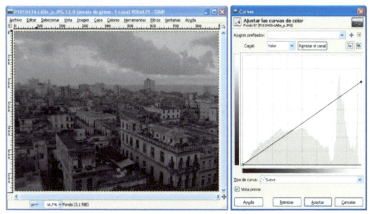

Above: white control point is displaced downwards

As a curiosity, you can try to open any image in your computer and the Levels adjustment. Now, move the black triangle to the right, or the white one to the left. Now, click on "Edit this adjustment as curves" button – you will get to similar results as the ones in this section.

Creation of control points

So far, we did not find anything new in the curves adjustment. We can do exactly the same as with levels, only in a fancier way, more graphic. But let's see what else we can do with curves...

With the mouse, we can add control points on the diagonal, as many as we want (in theory, up to 256, one per value). Initially, those points will indicate (as already explained) the correspondence of a grey shade from the below gradient with its output in the left one.

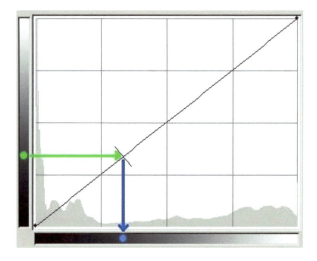

Now, we can move the new control points around the histogram, too. We will see that the diagonal transforms into a curve, which steepness will adapt to the performed movement to allow for a soft transition.

Again, if we move the control point above the original diagonal we are setting higher output values, thus a clearer image. You can see how the surrounding values are also affected as the curve is modified to the displaced control point.

On the contrary, if we move the control point below the original diagonal the output shade will be darker for that value and the surrounding ones.

As we add more control points, we can produce almost any desired complex curve. We can decide to create some control points and NOT move them, so that we fix specific tone values that will not be modified by the edition.

The further up or down you move the control points away from the diagonal, the more extreme the edition will be. In general, it will be preferred to make small changes, since we may be missing image information that cannot be recovered afterwards…

Usual types of curves

All the above said, we will find that usually some given curve "shapes" are most commonly used than other ones. Each one will have a defined behavior or a clear application. In order of importance, those could be:

"S" shaped curve

Produced with two or three control points, highlights get clearer and shadows go darker. Optional middle control point defined the range of tones to remain (almost) unchanged. Result will be an overall contrast increase.

Above: "S" shaped curve

"Inverted S" shaped curve

Also produced out of two or three points, in this case highlights are darkened and shadows go lighter. Middle point is also optional, in case we want to keep some specific tones unchanged.

Overall contrast is reduced. We will see later on that this may be a desired process when printing under certain circumstances.

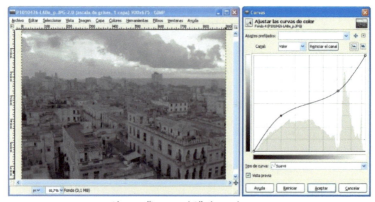

Above: "inverted S" shaped curve

"U" shaped curve

In fact, the shape is more similar to a "J", but this is the name that you may find in books and magazines... It is produced out of a single control point, moving it downwards. Now, the whole curve is under the original diagonal, which means that the output image gets darker.

Notice that both white and black control points remain unchanged, and so their respective tones. If the original image contained pure black and pure white, they will also be present in the output one.

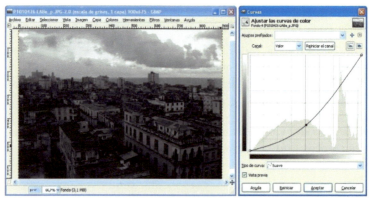

Above: "U" shaped curve

"Inverted U" shaped curve

The opposite effect to the previous one, in this case we move the control point upwards. The whole curve lays above the original diagonal, and thus the output image is lighter.

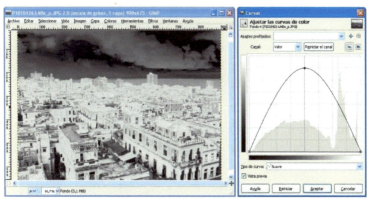

Above: "Inverted U" shaped curve

"V" shaped curve

Yes, this one should be the "U" one, but we do not want to mix them... It has an adjustment in two steps:

First, a control point is created in the mid tones, and it is lowered down to some "dark" tone. Then, black point is raised heavily (you do not need to reach 255, though).

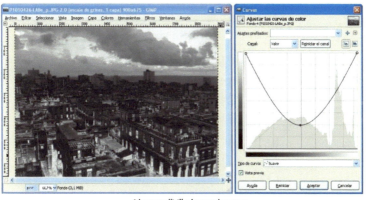

Above: "V" shaped curve

In this case, darkest areas transform into very light ones, as if we inverted the image, and mid tones (controlled by the central control point) will carry the image contents and look. The obtained effect is similar to the old solarization effect that was produced in chemical development.

Further types of curves...

Of course, you can work with as many shapes of curves as you want, or even produce some combination of the above. At the end of this book we will see a practical example for this – the basic calibration of a printer.

You need to take into account that every added control point will distort the original image information. You may reach a point where the edition is really a disaster – and you may need to go back.

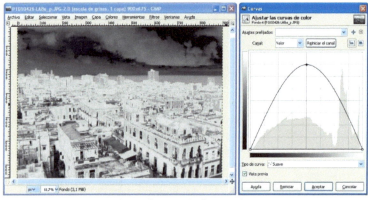

Above: "inverted V" shaped curve

This is the reason why there is a "Restart" button in the Curves dialog window. It will reset the image to the original diagonal, so you can start again...

> **Notice**: *I cannot stop repeating myself in these books. You are the artist, the editor. You must decide if an edition is valid or not. It is your personal preference. Of course, if you need to sell your work to a client, this is a different topic...*

Storing adjustment curves

Just as we were able to store levels settings, in order to recall specific parameters for later editions, we will also be able to save our own curves adjustments to apply them later on again to further pictures.

In this case, this will mean creating "your" own, powerful version of GIMP, which will allow you to work faster, in case you want to process a series of pictures with similar changes.

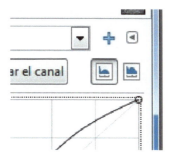

Again, you will find a "**+**" icon next to the (empty) drop down menu for "*Stored Settings*".

Practical usage of curves

In this section we will see (finally…) some real application of curves adjustments. I tried to order them by the complexity level – but don't be scared, we will go little by little…

Contrast, Exposition

As we saw in the previous section, curves would be the best option to make an overall tone correction in a given picture. We can increase or decrease contrast, make it lighter or darker, as needed. You know already how to do this with standard curve shapes.

In the above image (just as we did so far in all examples), we worked on the "value" channel from the Curves dialog window. But, in the same way as with levels, we will be able to work in each colour channel separately. Let's add some more complication here...

Colour adjustment

First clear application will be colour correction, or maybe the application of an intended colour tint to break the image colour balance, to produce some creative result.

For example, we can find images taken at dawn (or dusk). In portraits, this may add some nice skin tones, but this may not be the right effect if real colours need to be shown in the pictures.

In this image we have a slight yellow tint that we want to remove. Water looks too greenish, trees too yellow… maybe we did not expect this outcome when we took the picture

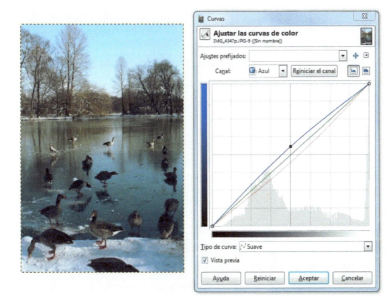

By correcting slightly the red cannel (to reduce warm tones) and the blue one (to compensate for the effect of the red edition), we can get more "realistic" results…

Duotone, tritone

An interesting effect is obtained when we apply opposite transformations to two different colour channels. A typical application is the creation of duotones, images containing two colours – that might not necessarily be black and white.

Best result is achieved from images in black and white, provided they are still in RGB mode.

> *Notice: If we transform a colour image into black and White through the command "Image – Mode – Greyscale", we will have an output file with a single 8-bit channel containing averaged values.*
>
> *To apply back any colouring effect, it has to be converted back to RGB with "Image – Mode – RGB". Initially, all three channels will have the same numeric values.*

To produce a duotone, one channel is left unchanged (maybe a slight contrast adjustment…), then the other two are modified with different curves.

 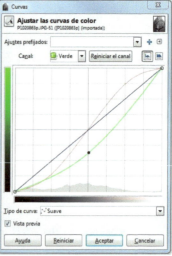

Tritones need a more complex process, which implies the modification of all three colour channels, so that we get different behaviours from each one on lights, mid-tones and shadows.

The result is a colour misbalance that may produce interesting results in colour originals, and brings back some colour to black and white pictures. Check the result in the following images:

Left: Original image. Right, black and white version with the proposed setting

Left: Original image. Right: Edited picture with three different adjustments per channel. Red and rose colours still keep their importance (this could only be changed by using "V" shaped curves, for example). Green tones are gone.

> **Notice**: *The success of a duotone depends on the public, who should be able to recognize the original colours and appreciate the difference...*

Traditional colouring

As already commented, if you find a nice curve adjustment (for a duotone, for example) you may save it for later recalling and application to a different picture.

Above: Three versions of a same image, with traditional colouring effect for Palladium, Sepia and Silver. Source: **Blanco y Negro con The GIMP**, Alberto García Briz

And, what if you want to mimic some special finish, similar to those traditional chemical processes? Of course, you may play with the curves tool, maybe with the "Tone – Saturation" menu... by try and error you may arrive to some valid result, close to your expectations.

However, most likely somebody did already do all that for you...

In the next page, you can find a table of the different values that you might use for some of those traditional processes.

Values are given in pairs (input – output), that you must set for each colour channel. You can see that this is a similar philosophy as duotones or tritones – but with given, fixed values.

	Canal Rojo	Canal Verde	Canal Azul
	63/67	63/62	63/47
Paladio	127/143	127/121	127/103
	191/213	191/191	191/170
	63/74	63/63	63/50
Platino	127/127	127/127	127/112
	191/191	191/191	191/175
	63/77	63/60	63/61
Selenio	127/140	127/125	127/129
	191/197	191/190	191/195
	63/59	63/67	63/67
Plata	127/119	127/131	127/129
	191/187	191/191	191/191
	63/79	63/59	63/33
Gelatina de plata	127/149	127/123	127/93
	193/213	191/188	191/156
	63/100	63/55	63/20
Sepia	127/165	127/115	127/83
	191/214	191/187	193/172
	127/24	127/137	127/220
Cianotipo	191/117	191/203	191/250

Input – Output pairs for the simulation of traditional colouring processes.
Source: Blanco y Negro con The GIMP, Alberto García Briz

> *Notice: The above values should be applied to images in greyscale that are still in RGB mode. But you might also try the adjustments in colour pictures…*

Notice that every time you move a control point over the histogram GIMP will show you the related values (input, output) where the mouse is. So it is easy to prepare the adjustment – it only takes some time…:

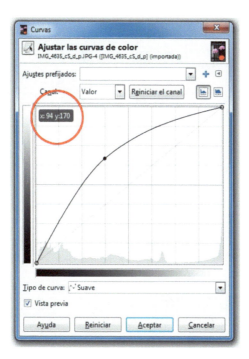

As you will imagine, you may save those settings in your local GIMP, so that you only need to introduce them once. If you like some special finish, you will be able to apply it to further pictures later on...

Film simulation

Notice: Part of the information presented in this section has been compiled from different Internet sources. Whenever it was possible, authors were contacted and authorization was obtained.

Traditional films included certain chemical products in one (black and white) or several (colour) layers. Specific composition for each layer and the very physical assembly made each film type and brand to behave in a different way in front of a same scene, even if camera settings were identical.

Left: Original Image. Right: Simulation of Ilford Delta 100 film, with the below described process. In this case, blue contents in the flowers results lighter...

This caused that most photographers picked their "favourite" film. If Kodak, for example, was known by the nice rendering of warm skin tones (for portraits), FujiFilm rolls produced saturated green colours, preferred for landscape photography. Other films provided enhanced contrast, higher definition...

As you can imagine, we can simulate (up to a given point) the dynamic response of these films, adjusting the curves or channels to highlight the desired colour. We will see some examples here:

Black and White

Black and White film used typically a single type of silver salts in the active layer, as sensitive substance to the light.

Depending on the specific composition and the size of the salt grains, higher or lower sensitivity was achieved, with different sensitivities to each colour (or light wavelength) inside the visible spectrum.

To simulate these different responses, most common procedure is to use the channel mixer in GIMP under "Colours – Components – Channel Mixer". In Internet you may find tables like the one below.

The values in the second column refer to the percentage of each colour channel to be input in the channel mixer. Remember to tick the "Monochrome" checkbox to get the greyscale version of the image.

Brand / Type	RGB
Agfa 200X	18,41,41
Agfapan 25	25,39,36
Agfapan 100	21,40,39
Agfapan 400	20,41,39
Ilford Delta 100	21,42,37
Ilford Delta 400	22,42,36
Ilford Delta 400 Pro & 3200	31,36,33
Ilford FP4	28,41,31
Ilford HP5	23,37,40
Ilford Pan F	33,36,31
Ilford SFX	36,31,33
Ilford XP2 Super	21,42,37
Kodak Tmax 100	24,37,39
Kodak Tmax 400	27,36,37
Kodak Tri-X	25,35,40

Above: Values for channel mixing to simulate traditional black and white films. Adapted from http://www.prime-junta.net

However, we might do a similar process (maybe better?) with curves adjustment and a later image desaturation.

Starting from a theoretical 33% percentage per channel, we can create a mid-point per colour channel and adjust it according to the above table, moving it upwards if the percentage is higher than 33%, or else downwards, if the percentage is lower.

> *Notice: This is still an approximate process that considers mid-tones to be the most affected by the type of film. Shadows and highlights are not modified...*

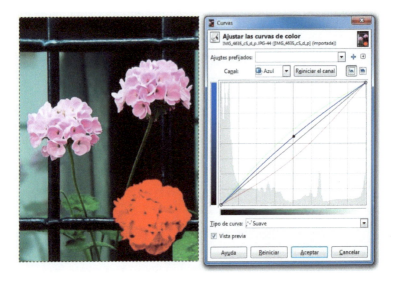

Example of curves edition (before desaturation), by adding a single control point per channel and using the same proposed values for the Ilford Delta 100 film, which is less sensitive to red colour and more sensitive to green.

Once the adjustment has been applied to the colour image, you just need to desaturate it (through "Colours – Desaturate" from the menu bar. You can see the result at the beginning of this section.

Fuji Velvia

But, from the previous section we can also infer that it is possible to play with colour images, too. As commented, every brand and film type reacted in a slightly different way to a given scene.

In case of FujiFilm Velvia, green colours were boosted, together with a general contrast and saturation increase. In "normal" vegetation scenes, results were often very nice.

However, in subjects who already did include a lot of colour or contrast the result could produce unpleasant, exaggerated renderings.

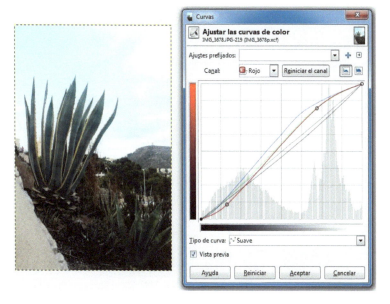

To simulate the behaviour of this film, three different "S-shaped" curves are applied (one per channel). Blue one is stronger in the highlights (and softer in the shadows), whereas red channel has the smallest adjustment form all three.

Fujichrome Provia

The slide variant from Fuji produced a great rendering for middle tones, with (maybe) a bit less saturation.

This way, the proposal here is to create an "S-shaped" curve for the red channel (slight contrast increase), another one (stronger) for the green channel, especially in the highlights, and an intermediate adjustment for the blue channel.

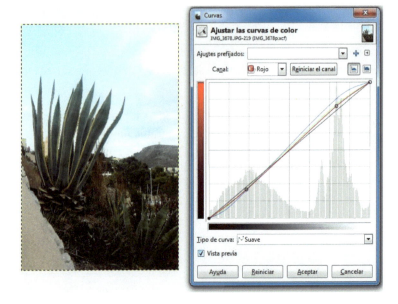

Kodak Portra

Developed to be a portrait film, Kodak Portra NC400 produced warm tones (ideal for skin rendering), with good detail in highlights while keeping contrast in the shadows.

We can produce the warm tone raising slightly the red curve in the mid tones and highlights; an S-shaped green adjustment matches the contrast in the shadows. Finally, a global S-shaped curve (on the RGB "Value" curve) will increase the importance of the clearer tones.

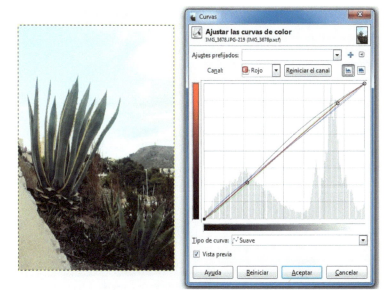

Cross Process

A lab processing that was very usual in the 80s and 90s of the previous century was the so-called cross processing.

In fact, this is not related to a specific film type, since it could be applied to all negative films. The technique used the developing process for slide films applied to those negative ones.

Differences in chemicals, development times and temperatures... produced an overall contrast increase and slight distortion of the original colours, which could end up really artistic... or a complete disaster. The advantage in digital edition is that we can undo the whole process, if we do not like the result...

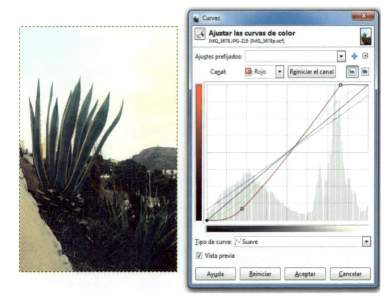

In general, red contrast was highly increased (blowing the highlights); on the contrary, blue tones had a reduced contrast in the output. To compensate for this loss of contrast, we apply an S-curve to the green channel.

Once again, recommendation is to store your "good" results before applying the transformation, so that those can be recalled later for a new edition...

> **Notice**: *if you make a quick search in Internet, you may find ready-to-use curves files, prepared by photography fans like you. On one side, this can help you in understanding how other work.*
>
> *On the practical side, it can reduce your workload quite a bit... but losing your opinion on the adjustment.*

Comparison between the proposed film types' simulation

Left: Original image

Center line, left: Velvia film simulation. Right: Provia film.
Lower Line, Left: Portra film simulation. Right: Cross Process.

As you can see, with a (more or less) complex curves adjustment we can give a totally different look to a same image... Which one do you like most?

Printing

In the chapter on Levels adjustment, we saw that a typical problem in the photography printing is the rendering of darker tones, together with the visual void produced in the highlights.

By means of the curves adjustment we can introduce slight modifications to our images upon printing, so that printouts are nicer to our eyes, and closer to what we see on the screen.

Black level adjustment

The use of pure black (RGB 0, 0, 0) can result in a saturation of pigments (either ink droplets or toner powder) on the paper, which can blur during the drying process, losing image details.

Then a good practice can be the application of an "output curve" as a last step before printing, so that the situation is avoided. To do so, we will open the curves dialog window (remember, with "*Colours – Curves…*") and will raise the black control point a bit.

This will cause that no pixel in our image will have value zero, but the selected value. As we saw before, the whole set of values in our image will adapt to this new situation.

White level adjustment

IN the same way, we also saw how the total Absence of ink (either liquid or solid) in clearest zones may produce unpleasant visual effects, if we are not working with high-key pictures.

SO we can try to lower the setting for the white point slightly, to make the

Loss of contrast…

Of course, if we raise the blacks and lower the lights we will lose certain available tones, and our image may lose some of its contrast. You may want, before applying the next transformation, first use an "S"-shaped curve to recover some contrast…

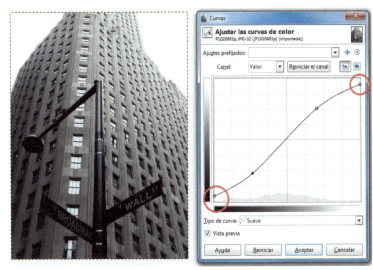

Above: Image with the proposed modifications for printing. This is a first approach, which should be completed with a printer calibration – which we will see in the next section.

> **Notice**: *Anyway, always remember that this is a temporary transformation, just for printing… in general, image quality will be reduced slightly.*
>
> *Store this setting between your favourite ones – but not with the final image!*

Advanced adjustment
Local tone correction

This is an interesting adjustment: we can modify a limited range of tones in our image (or in a selection, if you indicated a work area), by using several control points.

Two points would be used to set the adjustment limits or thresholds; between those, we would do the adjustment with all needed points.

Recovering the lion picture, I try to highlight the fur, keeping the highlights and shadows unchanged. First, I produce the two control points, which will not be moved around the histogram:

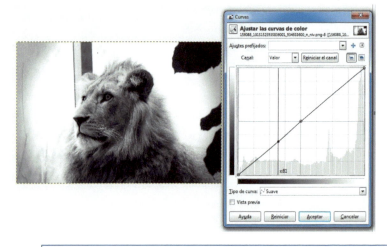

> **Notice**: With the Curves dialog window open, if you hover the mouse on the picture you will see that the cursor changes into a dropper: GIMP allows you to directly pick the tones on your image… the numeric value will be shown in the dialog window upon clicking.

The, I apply one more point between those to, in this case to create an "inverted U" shape:

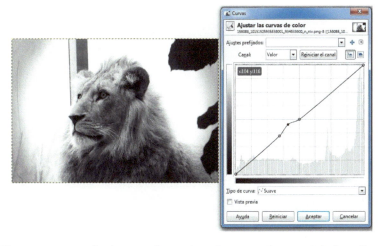

Now, we can apply the transformation. Compare the result below. You should be able to see the difference...

Left: Original image. **Right**: The selected range has been slightly lightened, without modifying all other values. You can see some more texture in the face and fur...

> *Notice: As always, it is better to make slight adjustments, to avoid the edition to be visible. Anyway, you might try some extreme adjustment — maybe you get to some interesting result...*

Of course, you can do this adjustment for different separate tones in your image. This will depend on the specific picture and the tones you want to modify...

Local contrast can be added, and it can be interesting to recover certain details in the shadows, for example. Or rather, the adjustment can be made to the highlights, so that some textures can be recovered in, say, curtains or bright clothes.

Layers, fusion modes

One of the problems with GIMP is that curves adjustment is applied directly on the very values table of the image, modifying the values. Curves adjustments are not an "add-on" that can be activated and de-activated.

However, we can work some way out of that – at least up to some extent. The way to overcome this issue is the use of layers and fusion modes.

Layers

Layers are "working sheets" for GIMP. On each layer, we can have full image information, which GIMP will overlay to show the global result.

You can see the information on the lower layers only if there is no information on the upper ones, or if the latter have some transparency characteristic. But this would just be the "normal" way to see layers. They work just transparent foils, one on top of the other.

> *Notice*: Here, an important difference must be made between pixels with no information at all and others with value zero (indicating black colour).

But there is a more powerful way to use layers, through fusion modes. Fusion modes use the mathematical concept of layer rendering (our grid of values…) and they perform specific operations with the values of two layers.

You can check the online GIMP manual at http://docs.gimp.org/es/gimp-concepts-layer-modes.html for an extensive listing of fusion modes and the applied mathematical operation. But here I will show you some useful examples and basic ideas…

Most important is to understand that the fusion (operation) is applied to the upper layer, but it modifies the lower layer.

To show some calculation examples, I will recall our 4x4 "image" used in the levels section. On top of that one, we will use a new one, with partial content:

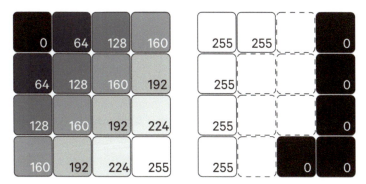

Left: Reference image. **Right**: Bit map to modify the reference image. It could be an edited version of the lower one, or rather a completely new one...

It is also interesting to know that there is an opacity adjustment (opposite to transparency) in the Layers window. By adjusting this value, we can control the intensity of the applied transformation.

Fusion mode Normal

This is the default working mode for GIMP. The image will show the information of the pixel that is present in the highest position of the layers' stack.

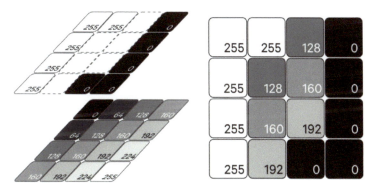

Visible result with Normal fusion mode. We just see the information that is present and in a higher layer.

So information on an upper layer will not modify that of lower ones, but it will cover them, so that lower pixels are not visible. Still, lower layers can be made partially visible with the above mentioned transparency / opacity adjustment.

Fusion mode Multiply

This fusion mode does just that – it multiplies the values of the pixels in the same position of two layers. To avoid clipping, the result is divided by 255 and then rounded. Since the division is made by 255 (maximum value possible), the result will usually be lower than the original one, and thus the overlay result will produce a darker point than the original one.

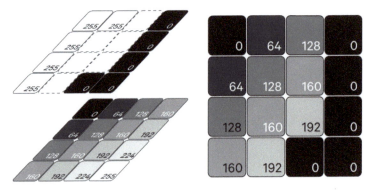

Application of Multiply fusion mode. Lightest values on top do not have much influence.

Fusion mode Divide

This fusion mode divides the lower value by the upper one. Math is a bit more complex, since some errors are avoided (for example, division by zero). The value in the lower layer is multiplied by 256, and it is divided by the value in the upper layer *plus one*.

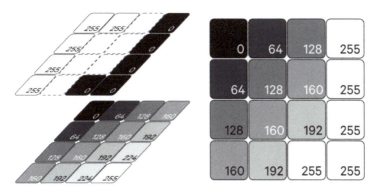

Divide fusion mode. Depending on the tones in the upper image, we can lighten the lower one.

Depending on the information in the upper layer (be it lighter or darker than the lower one), the behaviour of this fusion mode will be different. Anyway, since we multiply by 256 and then round the value, we will usually have a lighter image than the original one.

Besides, you must consider that fusion modes are calculated per channel. This way, an upper image with a give tint may modify the colour in the lower image, if the selected fusion mode is not "Normal".

Check the following examples to see how the different fusion modes change the result, using a landscape picture as base and a mixture of colour samples and text as upper layer. In the end, you will need to find the right fusion modes to match the result that you are looking for...

Some Fusion Modes examples

Source: Blanco y Negro con The GIMP – Alberto García Briz

Reference images:

Fusions applied:

Normal mode   Multiply mode

Divide mode   Difference mode

Colour mode   Soft Light mode

Using fusion modes

OK, so we can play with maths, do a fusion as complex as we want... but what is the use for that?

A usual way to work is to duplicate the image (usually opened as background image), apply any desired transformation (colours, curves, etc.) and then define the "impact" on the original image by choosing the right fusion mode and layer opacity.

This way we can keep the original image unchanged, to recall it again at any time. As an added advantage, we can hide or delete upper layers if we do not like the effect we achieved...

Ideally, we should create a new layer for each (curves) adjustment that we want to perform. Since the effect is transmitted from the top down, in the upper positions you should put the layers which should affect the overall image, such as contrast adjustment.

In lower layers, you should apply local editions, for example minor tonal adjustment.

A good practice, if you work with PSD or XCF file formats, is to store all layers information in a working document. Only when you are satisfied with the result you can export the image (remember, without the printer-specific adjustment!) to your standard output format (JPEG, PNG, TIF...).

> *Notice: This way to work is best option if you are working with masks and selections; else you will just apply several similar transformations, which you might also do with a single curves adjustment...*
>
> *You can also store different versions of an image in a PSD or XCF file (each one in a different layer), together with the original picture.*

One important note here: The effect of layers may be increased depending on the fusion mode. We saw that fusion mode "Multiply" will typically darken the image (when the upper layer has darker information). On the contrary, "Divide" mode will do the opposite.

So it can be a good idea to shift the middle point in an "S"-curve adjustment to gain control over the fusion on highlights or shadows:

Remember to apply the transformation on a duplicate layer form the original (background) image, which you can produce by right-clicking on the layer miniature and selecting the command "Duplicate layer".

> **Notice**: *A good practice is to give names to the layers as per the transformation applied. This way, you will recognize these adjustments later on, as the edition gets more complicated...*

In this case, we darkened the highlights and lightened the shadows. Remember, this means a contrast loss. In this case, this is not so critical, since we will use this layer as a *tool* to modify the lower one.

So far, we can see the effect of applying the curve in the upper layer, since fusion mode is set to "Normal" by default. If we change to "Multiply" mode, from the drop-sown menu in the layers window (upper layer must be active), we will now see the lower layer, modified by the upper one:

Outcome is darker, as expected. Now, we can control the intensity of the achieved effect by means of the Opacity control for the upper layer. I try a value around 30% - 40%:

> **Notice**: *You can see the effect of each layer in the overall image by clicking on the "eye" icon in the Layers window.*
>
> *This will hide or show the specific layer, so you can decide if you want a stronger or softer effect and if the opacity adjustment needs to be changed.*

In my case, mid-tones went slightly darker (with a final setting at 38%). Highlights and shadows were not affected.

Now, I decide to compensate this, by applying (as we saw in previous sections) an inverted "U" curve, in a new layer above the other two:

Now, I reduced opacity down to 50% since the effect of this curve was too strong (check the miniature).

We could go on with this process, adding new layers and adjustments as long as we want, considering that each layer will modify the overall result and information on the lower ones. We might reach a point where the added changes will go against previous ones… I would not recommend using more than two or three overall adjustment layers with the technique presented here.

> **Notice:** *Of course, the way to work with more adjustment layers is to use masking and selections – we will review them briefly in this book…*

Printer calibration

In a previous section, we just saw how we can correct the way that our printer does print our pictures. At least, in the darkest shadows and highlights.

But, what if all our grey tones come out somehow dark? In this case, we may need to work a bit more in our curve adjustment...

Again, it is important to have a properly calibrated monitor. You had better trusting GIMP's estimations when setting black or white points, or when making a first automated levels check. If you work just trusting your monitor rendering, you might be doing it all wrong!

Anyway, we will presume that you see "right" on your monitor. And you want to print exactly what you see on it. Well, then first we will do a comparison.

Black and White...

With GIMP, prepare an image with different grey shades. You may include the numeric value as a reference:

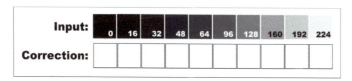

You should use about ten different values all along the tonal range. White is not needed, since we all know what it should look like – no ink at all. On the contrary, we might want to include pure black and a dark grey (for example, value 16) to see if we can get any difference.

Now, print the image and compare it with what you see in your monitor. If you see a darker tone on the paper, your computer will need to *lighten* that tone. On the contrary, if the tones on the printout are lighter than in your screen, you should *darken* them.

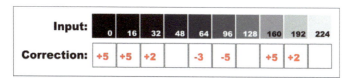

Prepare a table with the initial values and then assign some new ones (around five units higher or lower). You should have something like this:

Initial	0	16	32	48	64	96	128	160	192	224
New	5	21	34	48	61	91	128	165	194	224

Now, go to the curves dialog window and produce one control point for each pair of values, just as we did with the traditional colouring. First value should be your original one and then second value will be the new, target one:

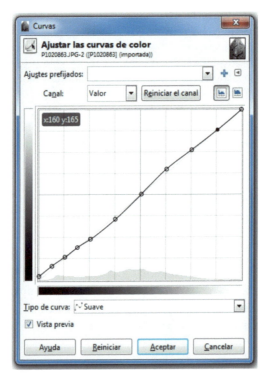

You must include all points, even those that are not changing (for example, 48, 48). In the previous capture, notice that GIMP is showing the pair (160, 165).

Before you apply it, save the curve as a draft. Now, click on Apply and print the sample again. Do not save the original image with the applied changes...

With the proposed (slight) changes, you may modify the behaviour of your printer, which will use different amounts of ink droplets or toner powder to render the different greyscale levels.

Now, make a new comparison. It should look better. Maybe there is still something to correct. Open the stored curve and make the needed update on the values which still do not look right. Maybe you need a stronger change, or the initial one was too excessive.

Save the curve again before applying it to the original pattern, apply it and print the pattern again... You should repeat this whole process until you reach a result that satisfies yourself.

...and colour

But of course, you will also likely have colour images. Maybe always. Even if you may get an improvement in your printouts, the above process can be too simple for you.

Maybe your photos have a slight magenta tone (referred to as "dominant"). Or maybe yellowish. This you can correct (just as we saw before) adjusting per channel, and producing a test pattern that includes the three RGB channel, as follows:

> *Notice: If you edit each channel separately, you will also edit the overall image illumination. Thus colour correction, if needed, should be done before greyscale adjustment...*

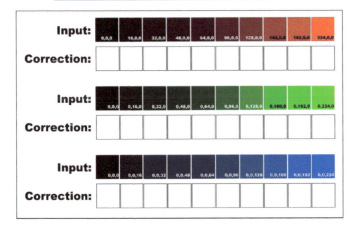

Depending on the outcome of your printout, you might need to concentrate in the mid-tones (say, between 50 and 200), or rather in the shadows. As you can see in the proposed pattern, the difference between values zero and 16 is scarcely visible...

Anyway, the process to follow would be similar. We would end up with a printer-specific curves adjustment, also related to our screen settings. And this would produce "valid" printouts for us.

But remember, you must not store these settings with the picture. In a different printer, or on a different monitor, result may be completely wrong...

Workflow...

An interesting point, maybe worth some (short) comments, is the work flow.

Through the previous sections, we have seen how to correct different aspects of a picture by applying specific tools. Contrast, lack of pure black or white, specific tones... could be fix.

But we also saw that many of these processes are destructive, they reduce the actual information in a given image. Formally, the outcome is worse – even if it looks better.

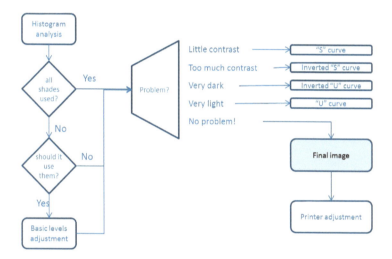

Main issue appears with "complicated" images, or if we do not know really what to expect from our edition.

Main recommendation is (together with the application of slight changes) the reduction of the edition steps to a minimum.

This way, if we see that an initial levels adjustment does not provide the expected results, it is much better not applying it, and starting a curves adjustment from the original image.

In the same way, if we want to apply a duotone effect, or a traditional colour, we should not apply strong contrast adjustments in advance, for those transformations will also modify contrast.

Finally, the adjustment curves for a specific printer should be applied as the very last step, and it should not be stored with the picture – except for the case where you only use that specific printer. If the change is stored with the image we can get to unexpected results, when printing in a different printer, or just when uploading the image to the Internet and watching it in a different computer...

Anyway, the definition of a work flow (the one presented above is just a proposal) will depend on the kind of images to edit, the final style that you want to reach... or even the kind of printing process.

You will need to work with your images to reach the process that suits better your personal style and working preferences.

Book covers...

In this last section, I will present an example on how to recover part of the image captured by our camera by means of levels and curves.

Of course, in most cases it will also be needed to work with further tools (selections, masks, dodging, burning...). These tools are out of the scope of this book. For the basic application of these tools, I recommend to go to the online GIMP manual.

Anyway, I will use some of them in the proposed work flow (with some basic explanation), so that you may see the potential of using several tools simultaneously: you might get a more precise control to reach, maybe, better results.

For the first edition of this book, I took a picture of a fountain. Colour version is quite boring. Colour does not add anything to the image, and the overall contrast is low. Still, there are light zones, some shadows, elements in the foreground and background... let's see its possibilities.

Starting point: The composition may not be the right one for this object in colour. In spite of direct sunlight, contrast is also not so high...

Histogram analysis

As I suggest throughout this book, first step is to analyse the histogram. With the original image open, I select the command *"Colours – Info – Histogram"*

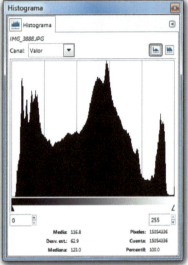

> *Notice: With GIMP, you do not need to move the mouse all across the screen. You have all menus available at any point of the image, by clicking the right mouse button.*

In this case, I can see that the tones distribution is quite uniform – maybe too much, which can be the reason (opposite of what you might think) for the "flat" image, not so spectacular.

There are a couple of peaks in the shadows, a bigger one in the mid tones and another one in the highlights. I can also see that there is no pure black, one of the reasons for the lack of contrast.

Preparation

Before doing any action, I will add some focus to the image, in this case with the Unsharp Mask (Under *"Filters – Enhance – Unsharp Mask"*):

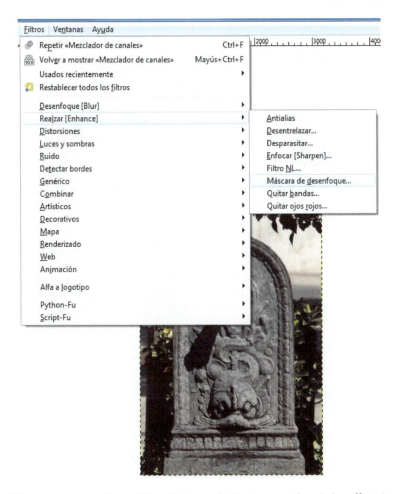

Since we are working with a high-resolution image, the slight effect is not visible in the screen captures in this book. However, this step (with the default values of GIMP) typically enhances local contrast and printing results.

Now, I will convert the image to black and white: As I commented, the little colour in this image does not add much to the composition – or even more, some details as the yellow leaves will draw the attention from the fountain...

I apply a channel mixer process, with 50% from the red channel and 50% from the green one:

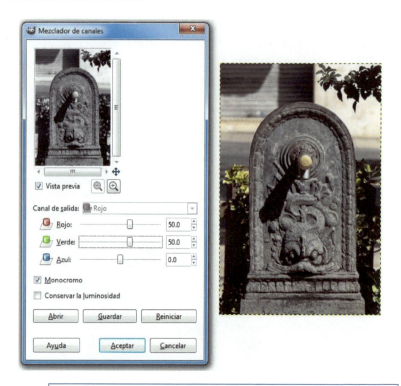

> **Notice**: *If you like Black and White, I recommend you my book on this topic, which details you can see at the end of this publication...*

Now, I check the histogram (if you have a large enough screen, you may have it always open) and I can see that tones have been redistributed.

In the resulting image we have darker tones caused by the conversion to black and white: some pixels had some blue contents, which we have eliminated, reducing their overall illumination value in the output image.

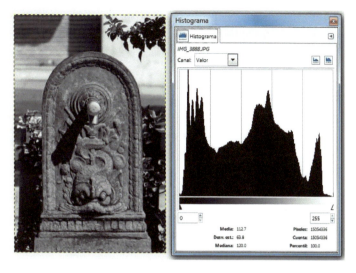

In general, all tones have been shifted to the left, and the new image has darker tones tan the original one. Notice that the highest peak is now on these lower values.

Levels and Curves...
Just as s check, I apply automatic levels to the image:

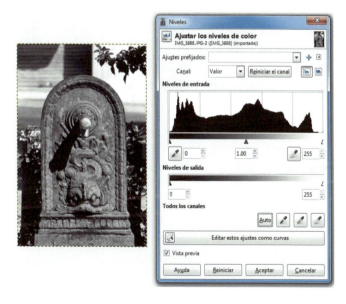

With the current tonal distribution, GIMP "proposes" an image that does not contain pure White. Since I have the dark leaves in the area where also highlights are located (so no danger of producing "empty" areas), I do want to recover the highest values. So I set the input white value to 245:

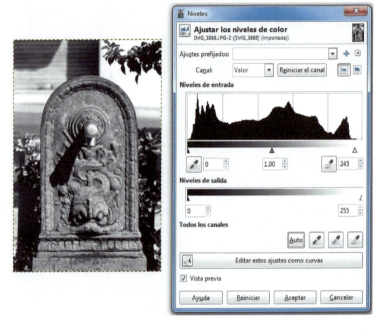

The result looks a bit better, in spite of (as we already know) having lost some of the image details in the highlights.

Still the selected composition gives more importance to the mid tones (maybe too much), the image looks too uniform. It is the lack of contrast that we detected from the beginning. So I apply a "S-shaped" curves adjustment, but off-centre: in this case, I have more tones going lighter, then just a few tones darker:

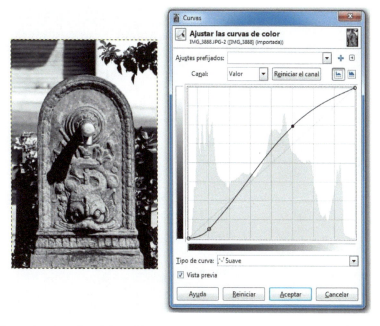

Pay attention, by doing this we are creating many points with "clear" values, which forces GIMP to make some rounding in the values. We will find that some values are missing; there will be no pixels with these values. This will be detected as loses in the histogram:

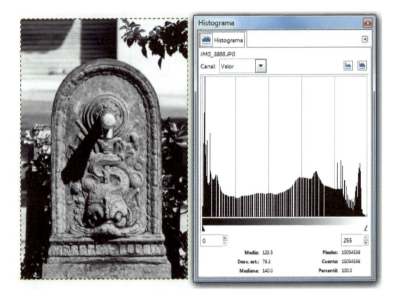

To solve this, I apply a slight blur (in this case, a Gaussian Blur with radius 1):

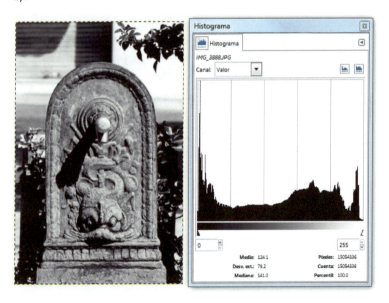

Now, GIMP has averaged the illumination levels, and we have some pixels back with the intermediate values.

> **Notice***: With this blur, we are losing image definition. This is one of the reasons why we sharpened it a bit at the beginning…*
>
> *Another tip here is always to work at full resolution, then only resize at the very end, so that minor faults can be removed.*

I apply a traditional colouring process. If you have followed the recommendations in this book, you may have created (and stored!) your won curves. You should be able to recall them from the Curves dialog window, by clicking on the small triangle on top right, and choosing the option *"Import settings from file…"*:

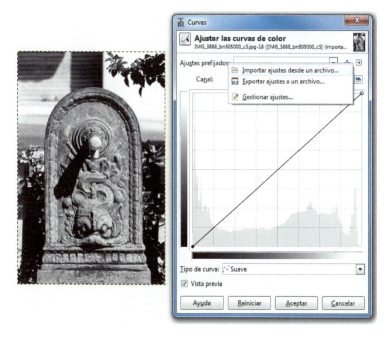

GIMP will show you the different curves available, stored in "your" version of GIMP:

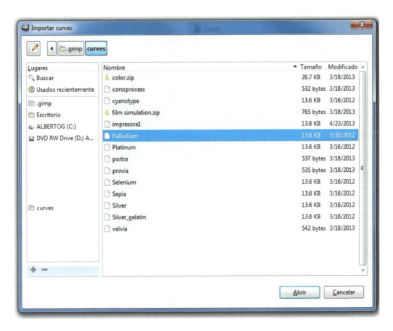

I choose the Palladium process. The result is the image that you can see on the original cover of this book.

Of course, depending on the final printing size, you may need to resize the image. In the case of the paperback version, it was edited in a standard size, 5.5 by 8.5 inches, so the image must be, at least,

5.5 x 300 = 1725 pixels wide

8.5 x 300 = 2625 pixels high

These numbers are proposed for a printing system that works with 300ppp resolution...

In most cases, the printer will request that you consider some losses in your image for the very printing process: Images are typically made bigger than the actual publication, to allow for an easier printing, binding and cutting process.

So if you are working towards a paperback edition you might be targeting (as an example!) real dimensions such as 5.625 and 8.75 inches – adding 0.125in in the exterior and both upper and lower borders. Calculations would be similar to those above.

Second cover

For the second Spanish edition, I decided to create a more traditional cover for a photo edition book. To do so, I would use a nice image that could draw the attention, with a dark background and a bright title that could be easily read, even as a miniature in an online shop. This point proved to be really important...

I chose a picture I took in September 2013, at the *Oktoberfest* in Munich. In this case, I was very close to the Ferris wheel, so I had to use a wide-angle setting. I achieved to get most of the wheel in the frame, leaving some visible sky above.

However, the direct sunlight produced very bright colours, and both the wheel and the sky appear too clear in the image. The picture did not have the "kick" I needed. So I decided to try a black and white conversion.

> *Note: For more information on the process described below, I can recommend my book "**Blanco y Negro con The GIMP**" (In Spanish, a translation to English is under preparation).*

Analysis

A first check of the channels information showed a much darker sky in the red channel (being red a contrary to blue colour) so the wheel contour was quite well defined. Structural, white bars had a high contrast with that darkened sky.

Blue channel showed quite a bland image, except for the red details in the cabins and the shadows of the roofs. Cabins appear, maybe, too dark, here.

Finally, the green channel shows also poor contrast, without any outstanding detail. White structural tubes and the lower clouds are the only highlights in this channel.

Decision

I decided to use the red channel only, but before making the conversion I will darken the blue colours first, to add some more "drama" to the final picture.

To do so, I apply first a curves adjustment to the blue channel. I use a "U" curve, quite strongly, to reduce the middle blues.

Then, I also apply an "S" curve to the whole image (Value) to increase the overall contrast.

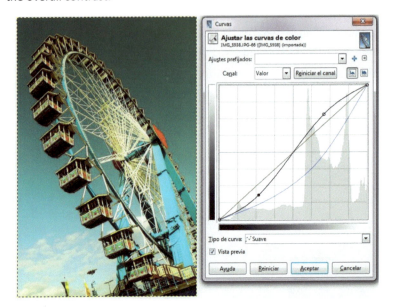

Note that at this point the original colours have been affected, so that the image renders somehow unreal. By reducing the blue contents, we are increasing a green shade, except for the areas with red details.

> *Note: This fake-colour image could have been a good candidate for the cover. Artificial colour gives an artistic touch to the picture, which might be welcome by certain public.*
>
> *Again, it is you the one to take decisions on your editions. This was not the effect I was looking for, so I decided to continue with the conversion.*

Now we can see the increase in contrast of the red channel. Green channel has not changed much, and blue channel shows darker tones all over the channel.

Before continuing with the channels conversion, I apply a sharpen filter, to preserve as much detail as possible upon converting to black and white. I use the command "Filters – Enhance – Unsharp mask...", with the default values.

Then I am ready to do the conversion itself, by means of the channel mixer. From the menu "Colours – Components – Channel Mixer...", I set the values as discussed before: 100% for the red channel, then 0% for green and blue. Remember you have to tick the "Monochrome" and "Preserve luminosity" boxes.

You can see the proposed configuration in the screen capture on the next page. Note that the result will depend on the selected original image and on the kind of finish you are looking for.

Both the planned composition and the book format were not so tall as the image, so I decided to cut part of the lower side of the image with a basic trim tool. New form factor would be more "square".

You can see the result in the cover for the second version. Of course, canvas needed to be extended again (this time, on the upper side) to provide a uniform area for the title.

Third cover...

As I started the translation of the updated Spanish version to English, I was not planning to make important changes to the cover. However, I needed to make the adaptation, anyway, and I found another good candidate for that: a picture I took at the Ammersee, near Munich.

A foggy morning, the lake could be barely seen from the pier. The resulting picture (my camera settings are usually fixed to neutral) showed poor colour information, and a reduced contrast due to the cast sky. Still, I knew I could improve it, so I decide to give it a try, removing all colour information.

Before converting the image to monochrome, I applied some sharpening to the image, to maintain some detail produced by slight changes in the colour shades. I selected the command "Filters – Enhance – Unsharp Mask...", and applied the default values.

Then, similar to the previous example, I made a channels' analysis, using the biggest miniature size that GIMP provides in the auxiliary window.

Both blue and green channels showed a plain sky, but the red one added some soft gradient to a darker upper-right area (which contains more blue contents in the original picture). All three channels showed similar detail in the pier wood, so I decided to keep the red channel only.

I opened the mixer dialog window with "Colours – Components – Channel Mixer…" and set 100% for the red value, then 0% for blue and green:

 Note that I activated the boxes for "Monochrome" and "Preserve Luminosity". Upon clicking on "OK", I obtain a first black and white version of the image. Still I am not satisfied with the overall contrast.

Then, I increase contrast by applying a curves adjustment. As you have read in this book, we are looking for a "S" adjustment, to increase this contrast.

In this case, I make an asymmetrical "S", so that more shades get brighter, whereas only a few, in the darker side, get even darker:

You have to be careful with this kind of adjustment. Notice that I darkened the low lights so as to have almost black on the boards on the left side, and the overall illumination is brighter, but still keeping some gradient in the sky.

Now, here we have another personal decision. That morning, it was very cold outside. The picture brings me memories of cold wind in my face. And I do not want to transmit that sensation (even if you were not there). So I decide to apply a warm tone to the image. Since sepia is (for my taste) too strong, I use a Palladium setting (described in previous sections), which I have previously stored in my version of GIMP. Remember that you can always make the manual adjustment.

Of course, the portrait orientation of the book required cropping the image to the proper form factor and dimensions. In this case, a 5.5 x 8.5in cover, at 300ppp meant minimum 1,650 x 2,550 pixels. Still, a bleed of 0.125in is recommended in the upper, lower and outer margins, so the final dimensions had to be 1,688 x 2,625 pixels.

Easiest way to work with exact dimensions is to redefine the canvas size ("Image – Canvas size…"), starting with the height:

I keep the most of the sky (losing information from the pier) to allow for space for the title of the book. Alternatively, I could have resized the whole image, to keep as much pier as possible, too.

> **Note**: Remember to flatten image after canvas resizing: this will reduce the effective size of your image file.

Then, I apply a new canvas size operation, to keep the required 1,688 pixels wide:

I use the button "Centre" in the dialog box as a starting point for the crop. You may need to adjust the position of the canvas crop before clicking in "OK". You can see the result in the cover of this book.

Levels and Curves with GIMP - Conclusions

In this book we have seen how we can improve our images with three simple tools: the histogram, to make a first analysis, and the levels and curves adjustment, to use the available tones or colours range to their best.

Levels tool allows us to make quick changes, maybe as a starting point for more complex ones to be done with the curves tool, clearly more powerful.

And, even when both tools are relatively complex and do need user input, the result is worth it, comparing it with the produced by automated tools and options – and, in all cases, we can start from the automated (levels) adjustment.

But, in my opinion, that is where the full power of these tools is: they allow you to do what you want to do. Not what some graphics application (or plugin) programmer expected you to want...

Remember, the decision on which adjustment is needed (or to what an extent) is fully yours. As an artist (either as photographer, editor or printer) you must find the process that suits your needs, and defines "your own" style.

And you need to understand it: more and more transformations may not lead to a better result. You need to know when you have reached the "best" result possible with an image, and stop there...

On the practical side, just as you need to find your own process and favourite steps, you will need to adapt your tools to it, saving your settings and calibrating your printer, for example.

And a last tip here: get used to store intermediate versions of your editions and do not forget periodic backups...

Glossary

Bit

Minimum information amount possible in computing, it can take two different values. Traditionally, those are referred to as "zero" and "one".

Byte

Group of eight bits, it is commonly used in computing (and thus in digital photography) for the storage and transfer of data.

CMYK

Acronym for *Cyan, Magenta, Yellow and blacK*, it is the colour system used in most professional printing devices – also called four-color printing.

Currently, GIMP cannot work with CMYK images, but we can make some approximate transformations on the colour picker.

Curve

Adjustment line that is applied to an image (or rather to one specific colour channel). It indicates a different multiplication (or division) factor for each different input tone or shade.

Duotone

Image produced typically from an original in Black and White, it is produced from two colours *different* from black or white. In this book, a simple way to generate duotones is presented with separate curves adjustments per channel.

Fusion Mode

Mathematic relationship defined by GIMP to render an output image, based on the information of two different layers. The upper layer is used as a tool to modify the lower one. Currently, GIMP provides 21 different fusion modes.

GEGL

GEneral Graphics Library, Set of tools and utilities with GNU license, which have been incorporated in the latest versions of GIMP.

Among the benefits, it will be able to work with 32-bit images, so that RAW files can me processed natively. Also HDR processing should be possible.

GIMP

GNU Image Manipulation Program

GNU

OpenSource Operating System similar to UNIX, launched in 1983 as an alternative to it; the fact that it was open facilitated the creation of different development groups, advancing fast towards the appearance of Gnome.

HDR

High Dynamic Range. Term applied to images that contain an extended value set, showing high detail both in the highlights and the shadows. Local "tone" is modified, so that every image area is mapped to mid-tones out of several images with different exposition values.

Histogram

Graph that shows the actual tones distribution (either light intensity or colour value per channel) in a given image. It is used to detect possible imbalances in the pictures, and to take initial decisions on the needed corrections or adjustments, upon editing.

LED

Light-emitting diode, Low-power semiconductor device able to produce light if a biased current is applied. Currently some television sets and computer monitors use this technology to substitute TFT panels.

Level

Amount of pixels in an image with a given value of light intensity or primary colour, depending on the analysed histogram.

It is a key factor as starting point for the levels or curves adjustment.

PDF

Portable Document Format – File format, original from Adobe. It has become a standard for generic document transfer between different operating systems.

PSD

Image file format, also original from Adobe, it was developed in parallel to their main application Photoshop. Currently, many programs (including GIMP) can work with this format, preferred because of its capability to store different layers and working data (masks, paths...)

RAW

Generic name for image files with raw data read from the camera image sensors, without any internal processing. They contain much more information than JPEG files – but their size is also much bigger.

RGB

Red, Green and Blue. It is the standard colour system for image rendering on monitors and screens, and it covers a great share of the visible spectrum for the human eye. Since a few years already, there are colour spaces derived from it, like sRGB and AdobeRGB.

TFT

Thin-Film Transistor. Technology used in the manufacturing of flat screens, it needs a white light source (and a grid of colour filters) to render the images.

Transparency

Characteristic of image pixels (usually, stored in s special layer, different from the background), which indicates if a layer, placed underneath, should be visible or not. All layers may have transparency but the background one. Some file formats (for example, JPG) do not support transparency in their layers.

Tritone

Image produced out of a Black and white one, it is produced out of three colours, usually different from the primary ones.

Traditional Colouring

Chemical process in photography that was performed on the paper prints with different chemicals. Silver salts were substituted by salts of other metals, achieving slight colour tones depending on the specific compound.

XCF

eXperimental Computing Facility. It is the native format of GIMP. Until release 2.6, it was optional. With the latest release 2.8, it is the default save format, and all other formats are produced by exporting. This file format allows for the storage of information of layers, channels, masks, paths...

From the same author...

Blanco y Negro con The GIMP (Spanish) - Alberto García Briz
ISBN 978-1478353911 (paperback, CreateSpace)
232 pages
Learn how to use GIMP in different ways to obtain black and White images with a professional look.
The different techniques are explained step by step through multiple practical examples.

Niveles y Curvas con GIMP 2ed. (Spanish) - Alberto García Briz
ISBN 978-1484813775 (paperback, CreateSpace)
104 pages
Learn to use these two powerful tools with one of the best free applications for image and photo edition. Second edition with extended contents.

Publicación online – hazlo tú mismo (Spanish) - Alberto García Briz
ISBN 978-1503186392 (paperback, CreateSpace)
120 pages
Self-publishing is a current trend in Internet. With a few steps, you can have on the table (or in your electronic reader) that book that you kept as draft for years in a drawer...
Fourth edition with extended contents.

Manual básico de Scribus (Spanish) - Alberto García Briz
ISBN 978-1499502442 (paperback, CreateSpace)
128 pages
Lear to use this powerful, free layout software to produce all kinds of publications with a professional look.

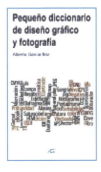

Pequeño diccionario de diseño gráfico y fotografía (Spanish)
ISBN 978-1500140748 (paperback, CreateSpace)
40 pages
Terminology used in graphic design and photography is, in many cases, too specific. This book will help you finding your way through them, when working with the different image editors, vector graphics software or layout applications.

Terms and acronyms are explained in plain, precise words, including, in their case, the explanation of the acronyms and their original language.

This small dictionary compiles and extends the different glossaries included in the different author's books.

Visit our web for further publication updates:

http://www.agbdesign.es/?page_id=5